To a dear friend,
    may you always find happiness.
              Jen Stark

happy

SECRETS TO HAPPINESS
FROM THE CULTURES OF THE WORLD

MELBOURNE | LONDON | OAKLAND

THE SECRETS

HAPPINESS & TRAVEL

Foreword by Maureen Wheeler, Lonely Planet Co-Founder

There is a famous story about two children who set out to find a bluebird; they travel all over the world only to find it in their own backyard when they return home. The bluebird, of course, represents happiness and the moral of the story is that happiness is found when you stop looking for it. Travelling to find happiness is probably always doomed to failure, despite all those romantic movies which claim otherwise, because happiness comes in those moments when you are not consciously trying to be happy. The moments of sheer joy come when you forget yourself and focus on something other than your own feelings or desires or goals.

When you travel to another country where everything is unfamiliar, your awareness is heightened, you notice every little detail because you are trying to understand and make sense of everything that is going on around you. The person you are at home, in your own environment, becomes less important, less central to this new story, you are an observer and this sense of being an outsider intensifies your responses and emotions.

Travel takes you to places in the world that are heart-stoppingly beautiful, exposes you to scenes of horrific deprivation and challenges you to accept and understand that the world is composed of both. But the moments that remain with you, when you look back and remember your wanderings, are those moments when you simply allowed time to unfold. Watching a sun set or rise, wandering around a ruined city or ancient temple, meeting someone who is as curious about you as you are about them, exchanging impressions with other travellers – these are all part of the everyday travel experience, and yet these everyday incidents will be the fragments that make up the whole journey, that stay with you and inform or change your perspective when you return to that other, 'real' life.

The opportunity to look at another culture, to see the world from another viewpoint, to see yourself as someone foreign, is the adventure of travel. The freedom, the sense of possibilities, the absence of the routine mundanity of normal life, is the excitement of travel. But happiness in travel comes from the moments when you are aware how lucky you are to be in that place, at that time, and how wonderful the world is.

INTRODUCTION

HAPPINESS. One word, nine letters, roughly seven billion definitions, one for each person on the planet.

Researchers are learning a lot these days about the intersection between emotions and neuroscience. Everyone's level of happiness is about 50% genetically determined (what the experts call your 'happiness set point'), a further mere 10% comes from external factors, and the rest comes from how we perceive our circumstances. Yes, money buys us some happiness, they say, but only to the point where we have security – a roof over our heads, a doctor when we're sick, a bit of entertainment now and then. Travellers take note: almost a dozen recent studies agree that experiences bring more long-term happiness than do possessions.

So, if we're so smart about happiness, why isn't everyone on the planet who has reached this level of security perfectly happy? Across the developed world, people have better medical care, fewer preventable diseases and longer life spans than ever before. In the United States, the pursuit of happiness is a constitutional right. But while many Western countries top the lists of overall happiest countries, many also rank highest in individual rates of depression and other mental health disorders.

The same researchers who study happiness will tell us it's not the flashy car or the new shoes that will make us happy in the long run. In fact, those expectations do us a disservice. Instead, they've found that it's some of the most basic aspects of life found in every culture that bring us the most joy – connection, mindfulness, gratitude, play.

While this book offers a few specific examples, these experiences happen all over the world in billions of ways: devoting time to honour family ties (p99: Tsagaan Sar in Mongolia), being still with the present moment (p43: *zazen* meditation in Japan), giving thanks (p33: Thanksgiving in the USA), or just shaking our collective booties (p109: Crop Over festival, Barbados).

One of the unspoken gifts of travel is it allows us the chance to open our mind, eyes and soul to how different cultures invite happiness into their lives, whether those countries are some of the wealthiest in history (p111: *hygge* in Denmark), or are struggling to put food on the table (p000: dressing up in Mali).

Whether you've travelled halfway around the world, to the nearest national park or a heritage street festival in your own city, you've probably felt it, that feeling of … was it happiness? Belonging? Joy, perhaps. Athletes might call it 'flow' and spiritual masters might tell you you've glimpsed the faintest echo of enlightenment. You might have recognised it in the simple pleasure of the Italian *passeggiata,* when you joined the entire village in the main piazza for a social evening stroll (p69) or when you became part of a group t'ai chi lesson at dawn along the river in Shanghai (p57).

So, does Lonely Planet aim to be the authority on world happiness? Heck no. We're still working on it ourselves. We know there are around seven billion ways to define happiness, but here are 55 we just happen to like. They range from physical pleasures like dancing in the Carnaval parades in Brazil (p91) to giving back to your community during the Chilean ritual of *'la minga'* work days (p113), or accepting the impermanence of life while building a sand mandala in Tibet (p23).

Experiencing other cultures can remind us just how much we appreciate taking the time to breathe deeply or laugh with family and friends.

Many of us have heard of the Japanese tea ceremony, but did you know about its world-away counterpart, the Ethiopian coffee ceremony (p59)? Like its Japanese cousin, the Ethiopian custom reminds us to stop and smell the coffee beans and enjoy time spent together.

Like *zakat* in Islamic countries or *jimba* in Buddhist lands, the tiny island nation of Tokelau in the South Pacific has a ritual of *inati* (p113), sharing their daily fish catch with those who need it most. And all cultures might want to take a lesson from Bhutan, where the nation defines success not solely by earnings, but by the population's gross national happiness level (p15).

When you arrive back at home, perhaps your life has changed ever so slightly. Maybe after a visit to Italy you take a 15-minute stroll before dinner every now and again. Perhaps you invite a friend over for coffee and just talk and laugh for hours, productivity be damned. Or, who knows, you might now start your mornings dancing naked in front of your cat to that calypso music you picked up in the Caribbean. But your eyes are now open and there's no going back, only passing on what you've learned.

MIND

IF YOU DON'T KNOW WHERE YOU'RE GOING, THAT'S WHERE YOU'LL END UP

SECRET PUT DOWN IN WORDS WHAT YOU REALLY WANT

Tradition **Shinto** *ema* (votive plaques)
Date **Any time**
Celebrated in **Japan**

So you want to be happy?

Happiness is an ephemeral thing, very subjective, and sometimes hard to recognise when we have it. Do you know what happiness means to you? Good relationships, personal achievements, material wealth? (OK, we all know money can't buy happiness, but a little bit certainly helps.) If you can't define it, you can't achieve it.

In Shinto temples throughout Japan, small wooden plaques called *ema* are provided for people to write down their desires and hopes. They are often decorated with pictures of horses (symbolising a gift), and usually cost a few hundred yen. Supplicants might ask for success in exams, a safe journey, a good outcome to a bad situation, or a new car. As each *ema* is completed, it is hung with the others garlanding the temple, for the *kami* (gods) to read.

The unknowableness of the future can be overwhelming. If you're feeling a little lost, try writing down a wish list for yourself. Think about how you want your life to look. What do you want to achieve? What experiences do you want to have? What kind of person do you want to be? Who do you want to share your life with? And then, actually put pen to paper.

Expressing your innermost desires in concrete terms helps them seem achievable. It narrows them down to a set of clear goals, acting as landmarks in the map of your future. Then you can start directing your first steps towards the place you want to go.

SWAP CASH FOR KARMA

SECRET PRIORITISE YOUR MENTAL WELL-BEING OVER YOUR
FINANCIAL SUCCESS

Tradition **Gross National Happiness**
Date **Every day**
Celebrated in **Bhutan**

Bankers' bonuses. Fast cars, flash houses, laptops, pads, pods and plasma screens. Life today is full of STUFF, and we're all rat-racing at breakneck speed to earn the money to buy it, to flaunt our wealth and success. But does money make us happy? Global economic growth has risen sharply over the past few decades, but there doesn't appear to have been a commensurate rise in our well-being.

What if our success could be measured another way? In 1972, King Wangchuck of Bhutan coined the phrase Gross National Happiness. The spiritual well-being of the people, he stated, is more important than the Gross National Product. The status of this staunchly Buddhist nation would henceforth be judged by the contentment of its citizens, not just the size of its bank balance.

Bhutan was beginning to open up to foreigners in the 1970s, and the king recognised the importance of preserving the spirituality of his people in the face of an encroaching modern world, and ensuring that capitalism didn't erode the country's core values.

And Bhutan is doing well. It has maintained its traditions (Argyle socks as national dress, a love of archery, fantastic folklore) and remains a largely happy place – though those breathtaking mountain views must help.

We may not be able to relocate to the high Himalaya, but we can still embrace GNH. Leave work on time to meet friends. Assess whether you're working to live or living to work. And place less emphasis on physical acquisition and more on massaging your mental health.

LET GO OF THE LITTLE THINGS

SECRET LET YOUR RESENTMENTS, WORRIES AND SADNESS GO

Tradition **Loy Krathong (Lantern Festival)**
Date **12th full moon of the Thai lunar calendar (November)**
Celebrated in **Thailand**

Sometimes it's the nagging memory of an awkward comment made without thinking. There was no malice intended but you're wondering if it might have been noted, and if someone thinks less of you now. Maybe it's something someone said to you that had no negative intent but stung nonetheless. Or perhaps it's something as simple as having to wait in line when you're in a hurry.

Turning these repetitive thoughts over and over in your mind till your head gets thick with anxiety – these little accumulations need to go somewhere…

Held in northern Thailand, and usually falling in November, Loy Krathong sees thousands of candle-fuelled paper lanterns drift away into the night sky, creating a warm amber glow as these symbols of worry and anxiety are let go.

As the lanterns float away, a surprisingly gentle, undoubtedly happy celebration takes place below. It's a simple act, but making these little burdens disappear into the air, perhaps combined with the beauty of their departure, has a powerful effect.

How can you do this at home? Why not start with something very simple, like writing down each thing that is irritating you on a separate piece of paper. Read each one, give it a moment of consideration, then make a ball of it and shoot for the wastepaper basket.

Or maybe go outside and let your inner pyromaniac loose for a moment, burning each symbol of irritation and anxiety, slowly and deliberately. Try practising cloud bursting, assigning each cloud a worry and watching it drift away. Ultimately, it's not how you do it, it's *that* you do it…

17

DIFFERENCE IS WHAT MAKES LIFE FABULOUS

SECRET ACCEPT YOURSELF (AND OTHERS) FOR WHO YOU ARE

Tradition La Vela de las Auténticas Intrépidas Buscadoras del Peligro (Festival of the Authentic, Intrepid Danger-Seekers)

Date November

Celebrated in Juchitán, Mexico

Being different can be rough. Most of us – from the seemingly perfect blonde cheerleader to the pimply-faced class geek – have at one time or another felt left out, unaccepted, alone. For gays, lesbians and transgender people, this sense of isolation can be especially acute. Though many communities around the world are beginning to learn acceptance of all people, regardless of sexual orientation, race or religion, we still have a long way to go.

In Juchitán, they're way ahead of the game when it comes to acceptance. The Zapotec people of the Isthmus of Tehuantepec believe in a 'third sex', a category that covers both gay and transgender people. Called *muxes* (moo-shays), they are considered a blessing to their families, and are accepted and admired for their beauty and domestic talents.

Long before San Francisco's Gay Pride Parade was so much as a gleam in a drag queen's eye, the people of Juchitán were celebrating alternative sexuality with a fiesta called La Vela de las Auténticas Intrépidas Buscadoras del Peligro – the Festival of the Authentic, Intrepid Danger-Seekers. At this fiesta, *muxes* dress up in colourful Zapotec skirts and hair ribbons to dance, drink and revel in the whole town's attention.

Imagine a world in which everyone, no matter how different, was so loved and honoured that they got their own party! Whatever your own personal difference, love yourself for who you are. And if you're not getting that acceptance at home, just remember – somewhere out there, someone thinks you're absolutely fabulous.

START

CLIMB EVERY MOUNTAIN

SECRET **HAVE A GOAL AND WORK TOWARDS ACHIEVING IT**

Tradition **Camino de Santiago de Compostela (The Way of St James)**

Date **Any time**

Celebrated in **Spain, France and Italy**

When was the last time you did something that gave you a real sense of achievement? Think carefully…

Coming up blank? Often our lives can become blurred mosaics of small triumphs and niggling disappointments. We put things off, we let ourselves down, things get lost in the rush. And with modern society offering a recipe for living that's half grinding stress, half self-gratification, it's easy to settle for easy.

The tradition of pilgrimage is common to many cultures, and continues to be observed in some parts of the world. In Western life, however, it has largely died out. A notable exception is the Camino de Santiago de Compostela, a Catholic pilgrimage with routes stretching from places as far afield as France and Italy, all leading to a church in a tiny Spanish town.

The Camino de Santiago de Compostela began in medieval times and still attracts flocks of devotees, though for many, the meaning of the walk has changed. Nowadays, it's often attempted for secular reasons, to increase fitness, to see Europe from a different angle, to spend some time in on-the-road meditation. Whatever the reason it's undertaken, most modern-day pilgrims report experiencing a kind of breakthrough along the way, a surprising epiphany that they never would have achieved without tackling the task.

It may not be possible for you to take off to Europe right now, but it's always possible to set yourself a challenge. Setting your eyes on that distant mountain and pushing beyond your limits to get there makes you realise just how, well, limiting the very idea of limits can be.

LIKE SAND THROUGH THE HOURGLASS...

SECRET ACCEPT AND CELEBRATE THE TRANSIENCE OF LIFE

Tradition Buddhist sand mandalas
Date Any time
Celebrated in Tibet

Human beings have a tendency to put themselves at the centre of the universe. Westerners, who often grow up in secular cultures that celebrate the individual, are particularly prone to finding themselves radiantly preoccupying and terribly important.

If we live in cities, we don't even have a star-teeming night sky to remind us what motes in the eye of eternity we really are. No matter what we do, no matter what we leave behind, time sweeps on: one day we'll all be dust.

Tibetan Buddhists illustrate this inescapable truism in a particularly lovely way, by making incredibly intricate, brightly glowing mandalas from grains of sand. The sand is skilfully poured from metal funnels to make elaborate patterns and the forms of fantastical animals, demons and spiritual symbols.

The sand mandalas can take days or even weeks of solid work to complete, yet when the mandala is finished, the whole fabulous creation is swept into an urn. Half of the sand is distributed among the audience, to disperse its healing through the room; the other half is fed to the nearest river, to carry its healing throughout the world.

Celebrating transience is strangely comforting. Spend an afternoon drawing chalk pictures on your front path, then watch them be worn away by time or rain. Lie on the grass with a friend making outlandish creatures from the clouds, observing as they change from dragons into ducks. Make a sand castle. Accept the inevitable truth that nothing lasts – and savour the peace that comes with it.

GET LOST TO FIND YOURSELF

SECRET LEARN TO BE SELF-SUFFICIENT IN ORDER TO FEEL
EMPOWERED

Tradition **Walkabout**
Date **Any time**
Celebrated in **Australia**

The modern world can make you feel helpless and ineffective. Doors open electronically, lifts take you upstairs and downstairs, meals come ready-made. People can be hired to clean your house, mend your car and walk your dog. Having so much assistance is convenient, yes, but it plants a nagging fear: what would I do if none of this existed? Would I be able to cope on my own?

Young Aboriginal boys had no choice. When they reached adolescence, they would be sent off on walkabout: a lone stroll into the outback for half a year. Carefree play was gone; in its place was survival.

For the Aborigines, this rite of passage was deeply connected to the land. Initiates would follow ancient 'songlines', or Dreaming tracks, learning to find food and shelter from the rocks and trees that sustained their ancestors. And in this quest, they would develop the deep self-awareness that only comes from solitude. They'd set off as boys and return as men.

Spending six months alone in the bush is neither practical nor essential, but everyone can take time out. Book a solo holiday – you'll be forced to fend for yourself, and discover what really interests you. Take control of areas in which you feel vulnerable. If you hate public speaking, sign up to do a course. Master basic car mechanics, or learn how to boil an egg. Gain confidence in your own abilities, and take comfort in knowing that you can rely on yourself.

TO ERR IS HUMAN...

SECRET FORGIVE – DON'T LET GRUDGES POISON YOU

Tradition Paryushan Parva
Date Bhadrapada (mid-August to mid-September)
Celebrated in India

Forgiveness is somewhat out of style. Tough guys would rather take an eye for an eye than turn the other cheek. Self-respect is used as a pretext for holding on to a grudge. Forgiveness can be viewed as a kind of doormat behaviour, or it can be cynically offered as the reward for an appeasing gesture such as a prolonged period of grovelling. Often we forgive only because the alternative is inconvenient or unpalatable, and it's the kind of forgiveness that doesn't forget.

Genuine forgiveness is something else altogether.

Forgiveness – one of Christianity's wisest teachings – is a feature of the Jain religion. Every year, Jains come together to celebrate a 10-day festival, Paryushan Parva, that focuses on various Jain virtues.

Characteristically for this exacting, austere but heartfelt and supremely benevolent religion, the festival ain't about kicking up your heels. Days of prayer and meditation culminate in a ceremonial asking for and granting of forgiveness. Only in this way, Jains believe, can you truly rid yourself of anger and hostility towards others and cleanse your soul.

In order to forgive others, you have to have the humility to acknowledge your own imperfections, and forgive yourself.

Try writing letters to significant people in your life, apologising for the times you've wounded or failed them (whether you send the letters is up to you). And next time someone wrongs you, why not surprise them by joyously, full-heartedly offering them forgiveness – no strings attached. It's amazingly powerful and liberating.

LOVE – AND TRUST – THY NEIGHBOUR

SECRET PUT YOUR TRUST IN OTHERS AND BE TRUSTED IN RETURN

Tradition *Castells* (human towers)
Date June to November
Celebrated in Catalonia, Spain

It seems we're becoming a less trusting society. We're so constantly bombarded with messages, it's difficult to know what's reliable. And as we become more ethnically diverse, distrust can grow from cultural misunderstandings. It's a sad thing, for a suspicious world is not a happy one.

The *castellers* of Catalonia have no such issues. The tradition of building *castells* (human towers) began in the late 18th century, when the folklore dancers of Valls, near Tarragona, ended their jigs by constructing small people-piles. This element of the dance became increasingly competitive, and soon a new sport was born.

The *castell* starts with a *pinya,* a firm base of many interlocking bodies – anyone's welcome to join in – on which the tower will rise. Subsequent human tiers are formed by *castellers* who climb up in a specific order to raise the structure higher, usually between six and 10 levels. The *enxaneta,* the tower's pinnacle, is always a lightweight (and brave) child.

The spectacle is a dramatic celebration of Catalan culture, with traditional costumes and musical accompaniment from the flutelike *gralla.* It's also a celebration of a community coming together, putting faith in its fellows to create something unique.

We can't all form human castles – they're impractical and a little unstable – but we can forge more open relationships with our friends and neighbours. Join a team – football, debating, tiddlywinks – to learn to work as part of a whole. See other people not as adversaries, but as partners who are vital to our mutual success.

THE ROOT LESS TRAVELLED

SECRET TAKE A LONG VIEW RATHER THAN EXPECTING INSTANT GRATIFICATION

Tradition Tu BiShvat Festival (New Year for Trees)
Date 15th day of the Jewish month of Shevat (January/February)
Celebrated in Israel

Technology can make things seem instantaneous, so much so that we expect instant gratification at the click of a button. No wonder we get frustrated when our lives move too slowly for our liking. All too often we lose patience, and sometimes give up completely on our goals when things don't turn out as planned.

Yet the simplest natural traditions can teach us important lessons about patience. In Israel, the Jewish festival of Tu BiShvat is celebrated each year with the planting of trees. Also known as the 'New Year for Trees', Tu BiShvat falls in January or February, depending on the corresponding date in the Jewish calendar, to coincide with the first budding period.

The festival represents renewal and hope for the future. Traditionally children sing songs about the almond tree and eat dates, walnuts and apricots. Aside from nurturing conservation, Tu BiShvat shows us how nature takes its time. Seeds are planted in winter, then sprout into saplings in spring, but it can be years before the first fruit is enjoyed.

Trees contribute so much to our mental and physical well-being, yet planting one requires discipline, patience and faith. It's a reminder that in life, it is far more rewarding to delay gratification and see our own efforts bear fruit.

Look carefully – are seeds you planted a long time ago starting to flower? Remember, you also need water, space and time to grow.

COUNT YOUR BLESSINGS

SECRET BE GRATEFUL FOR WHAT YOU HAVE

Tradition Thanksgiving

Date 4th Thursday in November (US) & 2nd Monday in October (Canada)

Celebrated in USA & Canada

Do you find yourself wasting energy trying to 'keep up with the Joneses'? In our materialistic world, striving to compete with our neighbours and endlessly wanting more imbues our modern-day lives with an all-consuming strain.

Instead of feeling like the world owes you more, try thinking about what you owe the world. In psychological studies of happiness, it turns out that gratitude is a key factor. People who practise gratitude tend to feel better about their lives, are more optimistic about the future, and they even sleep better.

In both the United States and Canada, one day a year is set aside specifically for giving thanks. Thanksgiving Day dates back to the 1620s, when the *Mayflower* pilgrims thanked God for a safe journey, a successful settlement, and a good harvest. In fact, so the popular story goes, the Plymouth settlers didn't have those things – many had died on the two-month voyage from England, and they'd arrived in winter and so didn't have enough to eat – but the local Wampanoag people provided food and seed that helped the colony survive.

Today, the festival is the most important holiday on the calendar. It's all about getting together with family and feasting, but still serves as a reminder to recognise the abundance in our lives.

But don't restrict your gratitude to one day a year. The key is to make giving thanks a regular practice so that it becomes part of your everyday outlook. Start a journal and write down one thing that happened each day for which you're grateful. Be specific: writing 'my family' is not enough. What did someone in your family do, and how did it make you feel? And don't forget, whenever you have the chance, to simply say, 'Thank you!'

DANCING WITH DEATH

SECRET COME TO TERMS WITH YOUR OWN MORTALITY

Tradition **Día de Muertos (Day of the Dead)**
Date **1 & 2 November**
Celebrated in **Mexico**

Death is a paradox: it is the one certainty in life and the greatest unknown. For most of us, thoughts of death are unsettling. It's not only our own demise that is difficult to face, but also the death of those we love. For some people, the fear of death can be so consuming it results in anxiety and depression, destroying all pleasure in actually living.

Over the millennia, humans have tried to cope with their mortality by creating belief systems and rituals. One of the most successful of these traditions is Mexico's Day of the Dead fiesta.

The festival's origins lie in pre-Hispanic beliefs that the dead live on in a parallel world and can return to their earthly homes. During the Día de Muertos, ghostly visitors are welcomed with offerings of food, flowers and candles, and feasting with friends and family. This is usually followed by a visit to the cemetery, where relatives' graves are cleaned and decorated.

Far from morbid, the event is a happy one, characterised by parades of grinning life-sized papier-mâché skeletons dressed in lively party gear, accompanied by mariachi bands and dancing, funfair rides and stands selling waffles. Shops fill with miniature skulls, coffins and skeletons made of chocolate or marzipan. All this celebration (and sugar) helps Mexican children grow up at ease with the concept of death.

Whether or not you believe in an afterlife, take a leaf from the Mexicans' book: celebrate your dear departed, keep in mind that you too will be remembered, and take the time to appreciate the days you have left. Accepting that death is part of the bigger picture and not to be feared is the ultimate freedom.

SING YOUR HEART OUT

SECRET FREE YOURSELF FROM SELF-INDUCED, SELF-LIMITING INHIBITIONS

Tradition Karaoke
Date Any time
Celebrated in Japan & Korea

Sometimes doing something badly is better than doing nothing at all.

Most of us aren't naturally gifted singers, just like most of us aren't world-class athletes, but that doesn't mean we can't enjoy belting out a tune or kicking a ball around.

Yet we tend to share a natural gift for rationalising why we shouldn't do something. These self-imposed inhibitions can cause us to miss out on a whole host of opportunities, and at the very least a good time.

Karaoke is an excellent study in shedding inhibitions. Do it Japanese style, with friends in a private booth rather than solo at the front of a bar, and it's a team effort to let loose.

It may seem odd that a culture with as much stake in propriety as Japan would invent something so potentially humiliating as karaoke, but the point is that there is camaraderie to be gained from the shared experience. When everyone has their heart and soul on the line, nobody is a critic. What's more, you'll find that the louder and harder you sing, the more your friends will love you – it opens the door for them to do the same.

Karaoke's enduring popularity all over Japan and Korea testifies to the appeal of socially sanctioned uninhibited behaviour. Even if there's not a karaoke booth nearby, take a note from the playbook and give yourself (and those around you) licence now and then to ditch the self-consciousness.

YOU'RE NEVER TOO OLD TO LEARN NEW TRICKS

SECRET KEEP YOUR MIND STIMULATED
Tradition Saraswati Day (Knowledge Day)
Date Every 210 days, on the last day of the Balinese
Pawukon calendar
Celebrated in Bali, Indonesia

Can you imagine going through the rest of your life never knowing any more than you do today?

Science shows us that the brain is a remarkable organ that's incredibly flexible and dynamic – our brains are meant to be stimulated! A lack of learning stunts our growth and creates boredom, while continual learning and mental exercise help ward off cognitive decline and depression in our later years.

Balinese Hindus regard our ability to learn and acquire knowledge as the most important gift for humanity. Paying homage to Saraswati, Hindu goddess of knowledge and learning, they mark their appreciation for our learning capacity on Saraswati Day, a colourful celebration that takes place every six months.

Children and teachers dress in ceremonial costume. Prayers for increased wisdom are made at schools and in family temples, and books at school, home and office alike are blessed with offerings of flowers and incense.

While the Balinese are supposed to refrain from reading and studying to focus on honouring Saraswati on this one special day, the tradition reminds us that there are no bounds to our acquisition of knowledge. The great thing is it's so simple to do: read a book, sign up for a course, or take a trip to somewhere new.

A commitment to lifelong learning helps you expand and grow. It gives you the opportunity to stumble upon new interests, develop new skills and uncover innate talents you never even knew you had.

Ask yourself: when was the last time you revelled in the delight of discovery?

KNOW WHEN TO BITE YOUR TONGUE

SECRET CONSIDER YOUR WORDS BEFORE SOMEONE TAKES THEM TO HEART

Tradition Chi Kou (Day of Dispute)
Date 3rd day of the Chinese lunar new year (January/February)
Celebrated in China

I'm just speaking my mind, we say – isn't it best to be honest? But if honesty is all that matters, why do words uttered in haste haunt our conscience? When trying to weigh the damage, we wonder if we could have struck a better balance between being right and being kind. Almost invariably, the answer is yes.

Insult or injury escapes our lips when we verbalise too much, too fast. The Chinese, who liken words to water (which when spilt, cannot be re-collected), honour that critical pause between impulse and expression by assigning the third day of the Lunar New Year as the Day of Dispute – a quiet 24 hours when people withdraw from interaction to avoid conflict.

The Lunar New Year, also known as the Spring Festival, is a celebration of abundance featuring painstaking preparations and zealous indulgence lasting weeks. But on Chi Kou (literally, 'red mouth'), all festivities are put on hold. People stay home to regain inner harmony or make their way to temples to pray, then turn in early for the night.

Next time you feel your emotions rising, inhale and count to three, or cast your eyes on the sky to get a sense of the world's immensity. Then, if you still decide to speak, speak slowly, and carefully consider the full impact of your words. You can almost always come up with a gentler and wiser way to phrase your words when you give yourself some time.

Oh, and get enough sleep. Apparently, we make better judgments when our prefrontal cortex is happy.

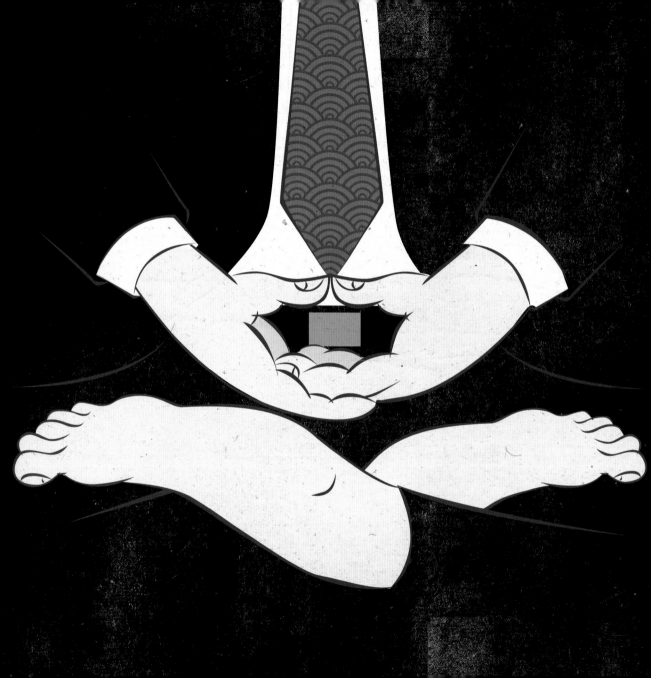

LIVE IN THE NOW

SECRET **BRING YOUR MIND BACK TO REAL TIME**

Tradition *Zazen* (sitting meditation)
Date Any time
Celebrated in Japan

We spend so much of our time with our heads in the past or the future, we almost forget that our physical selves are forever locked in the present. Too often, there is a disconnect between the living, breathing, feeling body and the eternally wandering, worrying mind. The pleasures of daydreaming notwithstanding, we are guilty of sacrificing the present for a place and time that we can never actually wrap our hands around.

Zazen, which means 'sitting meditation', seeks to bring the body and mind back in line. This practice is the keystone of Zen, a school of Buddhism that emphasises the experiential over creeds.

All you really need to know off the bat is how to sit – legs comfortably crossed and with your back straight – and to breathe deeply and mindfully. By concentrating fully on the act of breathing, the mind is naturally drawn to the present.

It's harder than you would think, leaving no mental faculties for nagging concerns. And as anyone who has ever sat through their first 15 minutes of meditation will tell you, time in the present goes a whole lot slower than we realise.

Over time, regular *zazen* meditation can give you a firm footing in the present and even reframe your worldview. Those first 15 minutes alone can help you reset. And while a quiet corner and a floor cushion would be ideal, we've found that just about anywhere works if you put your mind to it.

PICK YOURSELF UP AND MOVE ON

SECRET DRAW ON HUMOUR AND NEW EXPERIENCES TO
GET ON WITH YOUR LIFE

Tradition **Festa del Cornuto (Festival of Horns)**
Date **November**
Celebrated in **Rocca Canterano, Italy**

Upsetting experiences are inevitable in life. Take a bad relationship break-up. It's traumatic at the best of times, but when you split up because your partner is cheating on you, it can be heartbreaking.

The gut-wrenching feeling of betrayal, the shock, anger and sadness – all add up to a deeply painful experience. During life's most despairing and difficult times, you may find yourself asking, 'How can I possibly move on from this?'

In Rocca Canterano, near Rome, a festival is held in honour of those unfortunate enough to have had a love-rat partner. Actors parade through the main street, recounting satirical stories of love's misadventures, betrayals and break-ups. It's a wry, unsentimental take on the foibles of the human heart, with little room for wallowing in self-pity.

The parade's participants wear cuckold's horns atop their heads, a humorous nod to the fact that one's love life can indeed sometimes be a joke. The light-hearted approach and good cheer help console cuckolded partners, and festivalgoers seek each other out to ask if they'd like to *fare le corna* ('make horns' – something that probably doesn't need much explanation…).

You, too, may find it useful to acknowledge the bittersweet nature of love. You may not choose to don horns in an Italian village, but an ironic, philosophical perspective on life's ups and downs can help you move on from a relationship gone sour.

Take the first steps to mending your heart with some laughter, a shrug of the shoulders…and maybe some horn making.

LET YOUR 'BIG SELF' DO THE TALKING

SECRET SPEND SOME TIME ALONE TO RECONNECT WITH YOUR LIFE'S DIRECTION

Tradition First Nations vision quest
Date Any time
Celebrated in Canada & USA

Life's a rush. Sometimes you can find yourself carried along by it all, a jellyfish in a strong current. You've forgotten the promises you made to yourself when you were young. You're burdened by a morass of expectations and daily obligations. And those New Year's resolutions faded faster than a firecracker. What would it take to get back in touch with the part of yourself that has big plans?

In the First Nations tradition, a vision quest is a vital rite of passage in which you find your life's purpose. There are many different rituals, but most revolve around a time of physical preparation followed by a period of fasting and isolation,

often lasting days. During this time, the quester meditates deeply, calling on spirit guides to reveal to them the necessary direction of their lives.

Time alone is hard to find. To guarantee the you-time necessary to hear what your 'big self' is saying, you might need to get away somewhere by yourself for a couple of days. Go camping – or, if you're not the outdoor type, hole up in a B&B. At the very least, take a walk to the top of a hill.

Invite your deepest voices to tell you where you need to go in the next part of your life. The shape of your next few years might be a pleasant surprise.

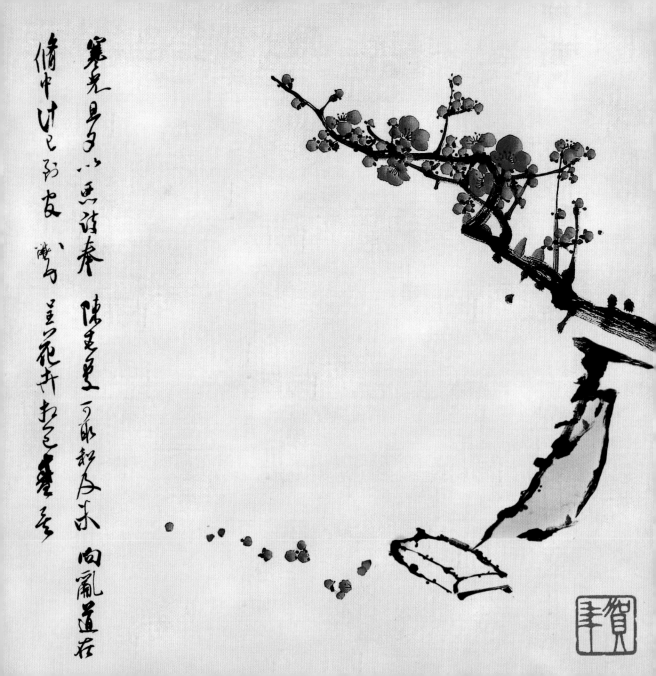

GET YOUR HOUSE IN ORDER

SECRET RID YOURSELF OF PHYSICAL AND MENTAL CLUTTER AND GET YOUR LIFE BACK UNDER CONTROL

Tradition Preparations for Chūn Jié (Spring Festival/Chinese New Year)

Date Lead-up to Chinese lunar new year (January/February)

Celebrated in China

There are times when things seem a little too disorganised and untidy for comfort. Chaos and clutter pile up – in your home, at work, or in that space inside your head. The unsettling feeling that things are spinning out of control begins to take hold, and it's hard to be happy about life when the mess is too much to handle.

Throughout China and in Chinese communities the world over, the lead-up to Chinese New Year is full of activity. The Spring Festival is a time of reunion, renewal and looking optimistically towards the future, and it all starts with cleaning house – literally.

Chinese families give their homes a thorough clean, sweeping out any ill fortune and making way for the new year's good luck. Households burst into colour with flowers, fruit and auspicious poems inscribed on scrolls. The streets are lit with lanterns and other decorations, and people greet each other with messages of peace and prosperity.

Starting over can include getting new clothes and a haircut, giving gifts and reconciling differences with those around you. Once things are in order once more, the New Year celebrations can really begin…

There's wisdom to be gained from these ancient Chinese traditions. You can make your own fresh start by revitalising and cleaning out those spaces cluttering up your life. So get organised and sweep away that junk at home, at work, in your relationships, in your mind – it'll give you a renewed sense of clarity and purpose, and might even bring on good luck…

RECOGNISE YOUR TEACHERS

SECRET **ACKNOWLEDGE YOUR INFLUENCES**

Tradition **Visiting teachers**

Date **The third day of Tet (lunar new year; January/February)**

Celebrated in **Vietnam**

Occasionally you find yourself wondering how you got to where you are. Even if you're OK with it, a little nagging feeling can become a full-blown crisis. Find a part of the answer from a period not so hard to recall: school.

Here's the thing: despite the horrors that school can inflict, you can usually remember at least one teacher who took some kind of interest in you, found some way of connecting to you that felt unique and special. For many, this teacher might be a clear turning (or starting) point. They taught you something that went beyond the textbook. Maybe it pointed you in a career direction. Maybe it just made you feel a little better about yourself as a teenager. Maybe you felt a little smarter.

In Vietnam, the lunar new year is the annual celebration of note. It occurs over three days, and is something like Christmas and Thanksgiving rolled into one. Days one and two are reserved for family and friends. But day three? Visiting your teachers! Teachers are highly respected in Vietnamese society. People take time to say hello, to acknowledge their presence in their lives (past or present), and to thank them, especially on this day, with gifts.

How can you thank someone who's taken you from crayons to perfume? It might not be so easy to visit a teacher from your distant past (though it couldn't hurt to try). So, a project: acknowledge the impact of a teacher in your life. Write about that teacher. Jot down the important things they said to you. What was happening in your life at the time? What would you say to them if you could? Is there a little insight now into the path you're on? As you do it, you could always hum a few bars of 'To Sir with Love' – there's something bright about that little tune...

FAITH CAN MOVE MOUNTAINS

SECRET ACCEPT THAT YOU AREN'T ALWAYS IN CONTROL
AND HAVE FAITH

Tradition **Prayer**
Date **Every day**
Celebrated **Around the world**

We all need to feel a sense of control over our lives. Yet there is so much that we can't control – the weather, the economy, death. Faith allows us to put all those worries on the table and accept things the way they are. What will be, will be.

In cultures all over the world, faith is rooted in religion. Counting rosary beads in Italy, bowing to Mecca in Saudi Arabia, inserting notes into the Western Wall in Jerusalem – through the medium of prayer, believers offer up their concerns and trust, along with their devotion, to a being who they believe has the power that they lack: the power to change things.

But there are no guarantees that our prayers will be answered in the desired way. The comfort comes, not so much from believing that the power to change things is on your side, but from the act of surrender.

Having faith doesn't have to mean praying to an external, interventionist being. It is our faith in humanistic values and an organised society that allows us to get on a plane and trust the skill of the pilot. It allows us to put our money in banks, undergo an operation, or climb a mountain.

When you feel your life start to slide off track, think about what you can control, and what you can't. Consciously let go of the things that are out of your hands, and work on those aspects of your life that you can control. Try saying a few words in private to God, whatever that means to you – to your guardian angel, your guru, or just to the world in general – and feel the weight lift off your shoulders.

BODY

STRETCH YOUR BODY AND MIND

SECRET EXERCISE TO PRODUCE ENDORPHINS, AND GET A PHYSICAL AND MENTAL WORKOUT

Tradition T'ai chi
Date Every day
Celebrated in Shanghai, China

You probably shouldn't have eaten that last slice of pizza. Or that half tub of choc-choc-chip. And lying in bed till noon to spend the afternoon in front of the telly is only adding to your growing sense of bloat and torpor. Your body feels less than top-notch, your energy levels are low and… well, to make yourself feel better, you might just have another slice of pizza. And so the cycle continues.

When your body's in bad condition, your mind similarly festers. Not only does exercise provide a short-term endorphin hit, but there's also an accompanying buzz from increased physical fitness that gives the brain a boost too.

Head to Shanghai's Bund – the historic mile-long esplanade that hugs the Huangpu River – to see this mind-body rejuvenation in slo-mo action. Every day at dawn, the waterfront flexes with locals practising t'ai chi: old and young alike stretch and posture in loose trousers, performing an ancient martial art as the sun rises on most-modern China. Some t'ai chi-ers wave swords; a few practitioners swoop fans, while others stand in a state of utter tranquillity. It's a slow, balletic display: a meditation in motion.

Try t'ai chi yourself – all ages can manage its subtle movements, and any practice space will do (though rising at dawn and heading outside may bring even greater mental clarity). If you don't fancy learning a martial art, find another sport you enjoy to get the blood pumping, the body toning and – as a result – the mind on a high.

THE FINER THINGS IN LIFE

 Tradition **Ethiopian Buna (Coffee) Ceremony**
Date **Social gatherings and special occasions**
Celebrated in **Ethiopia**

How often do you find yourself grabbing a take-away as you make your way home from work, or gulping a coffee as you rush to the office? Given that nature provides you with around 10,000 taste buds, you've got the capability to discern myriad flavours, but when did you last take the time to really savour the food you eat? Dining 'on the run' not only contributes to indigestion, but it also represents a missed opportunity for enjoyment on many levels.

In Ethiopia, the origin of some of the world's most distinctive coffees, such a frenetic pace is almost unthinkable. This slower pace of life is exemplified in the Ethiopian Coffee Ceremony, a 3000-year-old ritual of coffee-making that stimulates all the senses and is often considered a healing experience.

The ceremony is performed by a woman wear-ing a traditional white dress, who carefully arranges the coffee-making implements on top of freshly cut ceremonial grasses while attendees are enveloped in the scent of incense.

First the green coffee beans are washed and roasted until they begin to crackle, pop and change colour. A wonderful aroma wafts from the beans as the host grinds them and brews the coffee. Once brewed, the coffee is gracefully poured from a long-spouted *jebena*. Etiquette requires guests to consume three cupfuls of the coffee: the third cup, the *baraka*, invokes a blessing.

Life is too short to subsist on bad coffee and bland convenience foods. Try preparing more of your own meals, and invite family and friends to share them with you. Food and drink are one of life's simple but remarkable pleasures, so choose your favourites, slow down…and enjoy.

AND ON THE SEVENTH DAY...

SECRET TAKE SOME TIME OUT TO RECHARGE YOUR BATTERIES

Tradition Shabbat (Sabbath)
Date Every Saturday
Celebrated in Israel

It's easy to slip into a pattern where every moment of your time is assigned to some kind of busyness. Balancing work, family, friends and leisure time is tough – and when time feels scarce, it's difficult to take time out.

Rushing between job and home, falling over yourself to fulfil obligations, filling every weekend with chores, squeezing in exercise: when does the moment come when you stop to watch a bird fly across the sky or feel your own heartbeat?

The Jewish tradition of Shabbat, or the Sabbath, is the only Jewish ritual enshrined in the Ten Commandments. The tradition sanctifies a day of rest in imitation of the divine – for after creating the world, God rested for a day.

Orthodox Jews observe strict Shabbat laws that forbid such actions as turning on lights and driving cars. The day is often spent with the family, eating special Shabbat meals; a nap is not uncommon. The Day of Rest ends after three stars have appeared in the evening sky.

Despite the prohibitions, Shabbat is eagerly awaited and welcomed like a guest with feast foods, special clothes and spruced houses.

What would happen if you instituted the practice of reserving a day of absolute rest for yourself? It doesn't have to be every week – perhaps fortnightly or once a month – but it's surprisingly refreshing to allow yourself a day of blissful nothing. You might find it becomes your favourite routine!

SHED YOUR SKIN

SECRET **LEARN TO BE COMFORTABLE WITH YOUR BODY**

Tradition **Naked saunas**
Date **Any time**
Celebrated in **Finland**

Whose dumb idea was it to be ashamed of our bodies?

It's a rare soul indeed who doesn't have at least a slight case of physical unease when seeing themselves naked, that kind of 'I wish I didn't have such a…' feeling. And yet it is through our bodies that we negotiate the world. They are our finest instruments of awareness and connection, whereby we experience pleasure. Our bodies are… ourselves. Isn't it time they got a little respect?

Scandinavian Europe is famous for valuing physical liberty. Feeling comfortable with nudity – yes, even for those with less than model-perfect bodies – is built into the culture. Finland, in particular, is renowned for its communal saunas, followed by icy splash downs or snow leaps, followed by more saunas…and all without a stitch

on. The young, the old, the willowy, the wobbly – everyone's into the idea of a building up a healthy and invigorating sweat, and never mind the shyness.

If your culture's not exactly of the let-it-all-hang-out variety, you may have to take the quest for physical self-esteem onto a more personal level. An important part of this is to stop judging others' appearance. Try to see the beauty in old faces, plump bodies, eccentric features.

Now it's your turn. Try making a list of all the great experiences your body has been central to (your first kiss, learning to play the piano, eating that crème brûlée in Paris). Stand in front of a mirror and see the beauty that is particularly your own. You'll be well on your way to your first skinny-dip.

LET NATURE MAKE YOUR HEART SING

SECRET REALISE YOUR CONNECTION TO THE NATURAL WORLD

Tradition **Summer solstice at Glastonbury Tor**

Date **21 June**

Celebrated in **Glastonbury, England**

Every now and then, it's clear we don't always dance to a tune entirely of our own making.

We may get caught up in the myth of modern life – that we're all separate island universes, makers of our own destiny, controllers of our fate. But occasionally the irresistible power of mother nature takes over. Like when everyone's mood declines in winter only to uplift on a sunny day. Or when the urge to clean grips us like an eBay addiction in spring, or when other urges surface in summer.

Most of us will never know the optimum time to plant a lemon tree, or what soil is best for growing potatoes. But if we slow down and breathe deep, we can all feel the rhythms of nature ebb and flow within us, no matter how unknowing we are of its mysteries.

One way of reconnecting with the natural order is to mark the passing of the seasons. For millennia, pagans on every continent celebrated these transitions as the summer and winter solstices, the longest and shortest days of the year.

You might like to join the postmodern English Druids who camp out at ancient sites like Glastonbury Tor to await the sunrise on the summer solstice. Shrouded in mystery, the pyramidal tor is rumoured to conceal the Holy Grail, harbour an underground labyrinth and be a former stronghold of King Arthur. Whatever its human history, this old hill is a magical spot. So pull your blanket close and listen to the call of nature carried on the wings of sunbeams as they stretch across the verdant valley.

It is the song we hold in our hearts as we wander the city and stay up watching late-night TV. It is the music that will lift your spirit and set you free.

DON'T FORGET TO BREATHE

SECRET CONNECT YOUR WHOLE BEING – MIND, BODY AND BREATH

Tradition Yoga
Date Any time
Celebrated in India

Our mind and body are inherently connected, but it's something we often forget. Emotions can provoke a physical response – stress brings on sweating and tense muscles, fear makes us shiver or feel nauseous – and there is a theory that disease is related to a negative emotional state. But the converse is also true: we can use our body to alter our state of mind for the better.

The ancient Indian practice of yoga has many different facets and a highly developed philosophy. One of yoga's core concepts is the connection of mind and body through the function of the breath, or *prana*. Concentrating on breathing, whether performing specific postures or sitting still, keeps the mind focused on the body.

Deep, steady breathing encourages physical relaxation, and results in biological changes: our blood pressure is lowered, and resources that might otherwise be held ready for 'fight or flight' responses are allocated to the digestive, immune and other essential bodily systems, allowing them to heal. As the body recharges, the mind is stilled, leading to a sense of peace and happiness that's known in yoga tradition as *santosa*, or contentment.

Yoga is a popular activity worldwide, but you don't have to be a yogi to apply the principle. Using your breath to control mind and body can be a particularly powerful technique in times of pain or stress, as any midwife can attest.

Next time you find yourself strapped in a dentist's chair, running late for a meeting or in any situation that has you reaching for the headache pills, remember to stop, calm your thoughts, and *breathe*.

BREAK OUT OF YOUR BUBBLE

SECRET TALK TO YOUR NEIGHBOURS TO RECONNECT
WITH YOUR COMMUNITY

Tradition *La passeggiata*
Date Every day
Celebrated in Italy

Maybe it's the gadgets – being glued to your mobile phone, or so immersed in your playlist that you lose track of your surroundings. Maybe it's your work life – hidden away in a cubicle, or staring numbly at the walls of the commuter train. Either way, it's easy to get lost in your own private universe, and you end up in the same place: isolated and alone. Whatever happened to good old-fashioned human contact?

The perfect antidote to a feeling of isolation is *la passeggiata*, or evening stroll, an age-old ritual celebrated throughout Italy. It's a fail-safe way to ensure those face-to-face meetings that create true community.

As late afternoon passes into early evening, Italians of all ages throng the pavements and squares in every village, town and city, walking, talking, sharing a drink or gelato. For some, it's about socialising with old friends; for others, it's about flirting with a new flame. For most, it's all about slow-paced people-watching, strutting and preening, seeing and being seen. Whatever your style, the *passeggiata* reminds you that you're part of something bigger, that your community is there for you.

Taking an afternoon stroll with other people, Italian-style, can really pick up your spirits – both the exercise and the camaraderie play a part. But anything that gets you out and about in your community can do the trick. Volunteer, reach out to a neighbour, think about one aspect of your life that could be made more social – all of these things can help remind you that you're not alone.

FEAR LESS, BE MORE

SECRET FACE YOUR FEARS TO OVERCOME THEM

Tradition N'gol (land diving)

Date Any time

Celebrated in Pentecost Island, Vanuatu

Whether it hits you like a tsunami as you realise you're next in line to start your skydive, or it comes wheedling into your heart when your boss says you have to speak at a conference, none of us are strangers to fear.

One thing is certain: succumb to fear, and you're screwed. Luckily, the solution is simple. We just need to face our fears, then do something about them. Scary, but true.

On Pentecost Island in Vanuatu, the locals have a tradition that forces you to do just that. It's basically bungee jumping but using vines instead of an elastic rope. Oh, and you hit the ground. Because if you want the rush, you have to earn it.

The N'gol ritual involves stripping a tree, the taller the better, and building a platform to jump off near the summit. Ironically, it's only males who get to make the leap of faith, with boys as young as seven allowed to launch from lower down the tree.

It's ironic because as well as being a fertility ritual and rite of passage, N'gol honours the legend of a woman who, having hidden in a tree from her violent husband, tied liana vines to her feet before leaping from his clutches as he climbed up to kill her. Not realising the vines had broken her fall, her husband too made the jump...to his death.

Wherever you are and whatever you fear, climb your N'gol ladder, stare into the eyes of what terrifies you most, and launch yourself 30m down onto the mud. What's the worst that can happen?

READY, SET, PAMPER!

SECRET **ALLOW YOURSELF TO LUXURIATE**

Tradition **Steaming and scrubbing in a hammam**
Date **Any time**
Celebrated in **Turkey**

Do you have a problem with letting yourself relax? No? OK then, when was the last time you chilled out? Not just switching off or winding down, but taking the time to really relax, feeling it right down to your bones. Still coming up with nothing? Then you must be due for a little old-fashioned pampering.

When it comes to kicking back, not many countries beat Turkey. A centuries-old tradition of bathing – preferably in 17th-century marble hammams – gives it that special edge. Lolling around on warmed stone, sweating luxuriously, dousing yourself with cool water, staring up at a starred dome, perhaps summoning an attendant to rub you down with a giant mitt – can't you just feel your worries dissolving with the steam?

What, there's no bathhouse in your home town? There are still plenty of ways you can replicate the muscles-gone-elastic, blissed-out trance of the hammam.

Splurging on the occasional massage (or, better still, swapping one with your nearest and dearest) is an obvious but madly delightful way to relax. Make sure that there are plenty of fragrant oils involved.

If you want that genuine steamy feel, run yourself a warm bath and lounge around in the scented water until your fingertips go soft.

Or if that's out of your reach, pick a sunny day and lie on the floweriest, deepest grass you can find, letting the warmth sink right down into you. See? That's relaxed.

TURN DOWN THE VOLUME

Tradition Nyepi (Day of Silence)
Date Bali's lunar new year (March/April)
Celebrated in Bali, Indonesia

Life is a cacophony: people talking at you, phones ringing, children whining, advertisements blaring, traffic permanently roaring in the background, and on top of it all you've probably got an iPod stuck in your ears.

But noise pollution, like any contamination, is bad for your health. The words 'noise' and 'nausea' share the same Latin root, and exposure to a constant din has been shown to increase blood pressure. All that babble simply makes it hard to hear yourself think, to take stock and sort out your priorities.

The Balinese religious calendar sets aside the first day of the new year for silence and contemplation, to purify and allow for new beginnings.

After a night of wild partying, when Nyepi dawns after the dark moon of the spring equinox, all activity ceases. No-one works, no vehicles may be used, no planes take off or land at the airport, no electric appliances are operated, and everyone, including tourists, must stay off the streets.

The story goes that evil spirits will be fooled into thinking that Bali has been abandoned and will leave the island unharmed for another year. But the true spiritual value of the day is a time to meditate and reflect, to liberate the mind from worldly distractions, and emerge refreshed and renewed.

If you don't live in Bali you may not be able to enforce silence in your environment for 24 hours. Instead, find a private place to spend a few hours in simple peace and quiet – no activity, no telephone, no TV. You may find that the demons running around your head get so bored, they leave you alone.

A LITTLE SUNSHINE CAN GO A LONG WAY

SECRET **GET OUTSIDE WHENEVER POSSIBLE**

Tradition **Midsummer Festival**

Date **June**

Celebrated in **Sweden**

Being cooped up indoors gets you down. It might be through a long winter, during a spell of rainy weather or simply when you're glued to your desk to meet a deadline, but the result is the same: you end up feeling lethargic and listless.

A certain amount of fresh air and light are essential to our well-being. We need those sunrays to produce vitamin D for our health. And for some unfortunate souls, lack of exposure to an adequate spectrum of light is associated with a depression known as Seasonal Affective Disorder – SAD.

Is it any wonder, then, why the Swedes take to the outdoors with great merriment at Midsummer, celebrating the longest day of the year? The Midsummer Festival is scheduled on the Friday falling closest to the summer solstice, in the third week of June. Those living in Sweden's northernmost regions can even spot the midnight sun.

With origins stretching way back to early religious and fertility rites, the modern Midsummer Festival is a time to rejoice in the light and natural beauty of summertime. Families flock to the countryside to eat, drink, dance and sing around maypoles decorated with an abundance of fresh flowers and greenery, now at their most brilliant hue. According to folklore, elements of nature have special, even magical powers during Midsummer's Eve.

A little fresh air and sunlight can work like magic for you, too. You don't have to book a vacation or even wait for summer: just make a point of slopping on some sunscreen and treating yourself to the mood-boosting effects of fresh air and sun-induced vitamin D on a regular basis. Feeling better yet? Hello sunshine!

LET YOUR BODY DO THE TALKING

SECRET **EXPRESS YOURSELF PHYSICALLY**

Tradition *Céilí* dancing
Date **Any time**
Celebrated in **Ireland**

For many of us, a large part of our daily routine consists of sitting at a desk, jostling for space on crowded trains or getting stuck in traffic. And the faster things are supposed to move, the greater our frustration when they simply don't progress. Movement and emotion are so closely linked, all this inactivity inevitably leads to discontent, and the headaches, backache and stress that plague so many lives.

Since ancient times, dance has been used on ceremonial, spiritual and celebratory occasions. As a form of self-expression, it releases tension, boosts confidence and improves well-being. An Irish *céilí* is social dancing at its most community minded. It's not the ringlets and rigid arms of *Riverdance*,

but a raucous celebration of life where the most important thing is joining in.

No-one will glare with exasperation when you step on their toes; you'll just be dragged along in the right direction, spun ever faster and encouraged with a great big smile. *Céilídh* are all about the *craic* (fun), and it's hard to feel stressed when you're twirling around a room so fast you're afraid what might happen if your partner lets go.

You'll find *céilí* dancing all over the world but it's just one way of strutting your stuff. You can turn up the music and prance around your bedroom in your undies, hit your local nightclub, join a salsa class, sway, slide, wriggle or rock. It doesn't have to cost a thing, and is guaranteed to make you smile.

DISCIPLINE IS NOT A DIRTY WORD

Tradition **Ramadan**
Date **The ninth month of the Islamic lunar calendar**
Celebrated in **Egypt**

Whether we're talking possessions or the latest food fads, it seems we can never have enough. Bombarded with pleas to buy the hottest gadgets, must-have new toys and best value-for-money meal combo with the lot, it's easy to fall prey to overindulgence and excessive consumption.

Wouldn't it be good to stop and take stock? For one month every year, Muslims in Egypt and across the world do just that, turning the tables on the pursuit of more and being prepared to go without. From dawn to dusk during the holy month of Ramadan, not a morsel of food or a drop of water will pass the lips of Egyptian Muslims as a reminder of how lucky they are to possess what they have.

It is a time of deep reflection on the blessings of life, where all – rich and poor, young and old – become equal. Ramadan evenings are an especially joyous occasion across Egypt. Great feasts are prepared, and family and loved ones gather to enjoy life's simple pleasures of drinking and eating after the long day of fasting.

You don't need to be a Muslim to carry out a fast. But if it all seems too extreme, why not deny yourself that extra cappuccino or muffin for a month, and put the money saved towards a favourite good cause. You'll soon find yourself smiling at the multitude of blessings you actually have.

YOU ARE WHAT YOU WEAR

SECRET DRESS YOURSELF UP TO CREATE BEAUTY WHERE YOU SEE NONE

Tradition Dressing up, Soninke style
Date Any time
Celebrated in Mali, Niger & eastern Senegal

When your world, or just your day, falls apart, it can be easy to fall apart with it. Whatever sparked it – tough times at work, a big disappointment, heartbreak or drastic change – you're not in a happy place.

When things look sad and monotonous, take a step back. There's room for beauty, too, in sadness, and if you can't find it, you can always create it.

In the Sahel region of Africa, nomadic groups such as the Soninke, subsets of the Fulani and the Wodaabe, spend their days traversing the desolate landscape of scrubland and sun-seared desert, their belongings piled high on the skinny haunches of donkeys. In the dry season, the heat is scalding. In the wet, it's a suffocating, clammy hand around the neck.

But how pretty they look! Gold hoops are laced five-fold through ears. Dresses are long and red and graceful. Hair is braided with pink and silver, and eyes are lined with a blue brighter than the midday sky. Juxtaposed against the lonely landscapes, the Wodaabe women in particular can show us a thing or two about beauty.

When you already feel lost in no-man's land, there's no sense boarding a flight to Timbuktu. Even if you have no intention of leaving the house, raid your jewellery box and throw on a pair of sparkles, go shopping in the back of your own closet or dig out that shade of red lipstick you bought for a special occasion – this is it. Don't fade into your surroundings. That tough place you're in right now? It's not you. It's just a place.

TALK ABOUT IT

SECRET **GET THINGS OFF YOUR CHEST WITH LIKE-MINDED OTHERS**

Tradition *Stammtisch* (regulars' table)

Date **Any time**

Celebrated in **Germany**

You think football is the most important thing in the world. Or you've just had a baby and it's changed your entire life. But the people around you don't want to know! Maybe the daily grind is dulling their curiosity and engendering a little groupthink, or maybe they just don't share your interests and find your enthusiasm a little weird. Either way, you need to find new people to talk to.

In Germany, friends, colleagues and interested strangers get together regularly at *Stammtisches* to chat, laugh, spark connections and get a fresh perspective on the subjects that interest them. Historically, these informal gatherings were only open to the town's elite, who would share local news over drinks at a reserved table at the local restaurant or pub.

Since the 1990s, *Stammtisches* have become a way for groups of people with common passions or hobbies to meet up and talk. Groups have formed all over Germany, around every subject imaginable, from professions to politics to languages to parenthood, giving participants the chance to discuss their experiences, network and express whatever is on their minds. The people you meet at *Stammtisch* groups seldom stay strangers for long.

Forging connections over a common interest gives you the warm glow of camaraderie and bonding. Why not book a table somewhere and give a few like-minded friends a call? Ask them to invite friends of their own, put some posters up around town, spread the word online, and before long, the conversation will be flowing as fast as the beer.

TEST YOUR LIMITS TO TRANSCEND YOUR SELF

SECRET **DISCOVER WHAT'S DEEP INSIDE WITH A PHYSICAL CHALLENGE**

Tradition **Self-transcendence marathon**
Date **June to August**
Celebrated in **Queens, New York City, USA**

Ask yourself: how often do you tackle something physically challenging?

Maybe you run, or work out in the gym. You know that a good session clears your mind: makes you feel light and free. Perhaps being physical helps you find clarity and still those noisy thoughts in your head. But what about taking on something so physically and mentally difficult, you don't know whether you'll be capable? Might that be a way to go deeper inside than you've ever gone before?

Each year, an unremarkable city block in Queens becomes the backdrop for an entirely re-markable challenge: the 4988km (3100-mile) Self-Transcendence Marathon – the longest foot-race in the world. Runners must complete the equivalent of two full marathons (84km/52 miles) each day to cover the distance within the 52-day limit. In the heat of summer, from sunrise to midnight, participants circuit a half-mile block up to 100 times daily.

Founded by Indian spiritual teacher Sri Chinmoy, who prescribed extraordinary physical and mental feats to expand the mind, the race is the ultimate test of survival and endurance. The marathon is a struggle for both the body and the mind, in which participants must truly transcend themselves.

But there's no need to run a thousand miles. The spirit of this challenge is to gain self-knowledge by achieving something that's difficult, *for you*. Whatever your goal, realising it will give you a new certainty that you can overcome your own perceived limits. You may even find a strength deep within yourself that makes almost anything seem possible.

SPIRIT

LET LOOSE

Tradition **Carnaval**
Date **February or March**
Celebrated in **Brazil**

All work and no play makes Jack and Jill a dull boy and girl – and stressed-out ones too!

In a world that's open for business 24/7 and measures well-being by the bottom line, it's sometimes easy to feel like a dutiful drudge, with no room to kick up your heels. But what if you could bring the workaday world to a screeching halt? What if there was an entire week when your culture asked you to drop everything and simply celebrate being alive?

For the five days leading up to Ash Wednesday, Brazil's annual Carnaval is just such a party. Business as usual is shut down for almost a solid week, the entire social order is flipped on its head, and everybody is reminded that the things that really matter in life can't be measured on spreadsheets.

Blending African beats, Native American–inspired costumes and Bacchanalian traditions with roots in ancient Europe, Carnaval is a euphoric celebration of Brazil's diversity and openness to creative self-expression. It's an exuberant, non-stop frenzy of music, dancing and sensuality that involves the whole community. With businesses and banks shuttered from Friday to Ash Wednesday, there's no excuse not to be out having fun.

Even if you can't make it to Brazil, you can join carnival festivities closer to home. Or why not get together with friends and plot your own creative release? Whatever you do, find a way to let go of the status quo for a few days every year. Without a doubt, these are the times you'll remember on your deathbed, not your regular nine to five.

LAUGH IT OFF

SECRET **TAKE LIFE LESS SERIOUSLY**

Tradition **Hasya yoga (laughter therapy)**
Date **Any time**
Celebrated in **India**

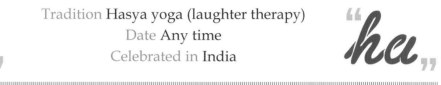

Perhaps it's a scowl from a colleague. Or a snide remark from someone at your school reunion. Maybe it's discovering yet another papery wrinkle on your once-smooth forehead. Or lamenting a lost opportunity. Whatever it may be, we are masters of dwelling on negative thoughts, allowing them to steamroll our self-esteem and mess with our minds. Life, circa Now, is no laughing matter. But should it be?

Starting with chants of 'Ho Ho Ha Ha' and culminating in deep belly guffaws, the Indian practice of Hasya yoga recognises the potent physical and emotional healing properties of a good giggle. The health benefits apply regardless of whether or not the laughter is genuine, and therein lies the medicinal magic – and remarkable simplicity – of Hasya yoga, or laughter therapy.

Don't snigger. Recent reports indicate that adults laugh, on average, 15 times per day – a grim statistic when compared to the childhood average of 350. Grim because laughter has been scientifically proven to significantly enhance our overall well-being: it relaxes muscles, triggers the release of 'happy' hormones, clears respiratory passages, helps strengthen the cardiovascular system, boosts immune function and radically elevates mood. No wonder Hasya yoga has gone global.

Turn your frown upside down. Write on a piece of paper 'Laughter is the best medicine', stick it on your fridge and make it a point to greet each day with a jolly good chuckle. Stretch your arms in the air, close your eyes, take some deep breaths, then Ho Ho Ha Ha your way to a much happier, healthier you.

HOME IS WHERE THE EARTH IS

SECRET REALISE YOUR CONNECTION TO PLACE

Tradition Garma Festival
Date Early August
Celebrated in Gulkula, northeast Arnhem Land, Australia

Ever felt a sense of disconnection? Felt out of time and out of place?

When this happens, it's good to remember the fixed points in life. Those things that remain constant, like memories or notions of home. That sense of place that calls to us and that we continue to call our own. For when we need reassurance, we tend to look back, to the past. Somehow, the past is always present, shaping us and leading us forward.

Each August, during the comparative cool of the tropical winter, the Yolngu people of northeast Arnhem Land come together to reconnect to place during the four-day Garma Festival. The festival is held in a stringybark forest, where the ancestral didgeridoo was brought to the Yolngu. It's a land criss-crossed by traditional songlines, those tracks and sites where ancestor beings called the country into existence.

The Yolngu people's connection with country is tangible. It's in the shades of ochre on skin, the feel and taste of dust kicked up from dancers' feet; the pervasive sound of the didgeridoo and smell of the stringybarks. It seems both very ancient and entirely contemporary – a kind of looking back to the future, perhaps.

Connections can be made by any of us, anywhere. It's partly about paying attention. See that nearby tree in the garden or bush or city park? Watch it over time. Notice its – and your – response as seasons pass. And, as the world moves on, begin to feel more connected; more at home.

SPRING-CLEAN MIND, BODY AND SPIRIT

SECRET **WASH AWAY THE OLD AND WELCOME THE NEW**

Tradition **Songkran (Thai New Year)**
Date **13 to 15 April**
Celebrated in **Thailand**

Time slips away like water.

One minute we're making New Year's resolutions, the next we're wondering where the year went. Everyday worries, duties and work stresses sweep us along in their current and slowly but surely drain us of energy. If only we could wipe the slate clean and start afresh.

Songkran, or Thai New Year, celebrates the sun moving into Aries with the ultimate spring clean of mind, body and spirit. On the face of things, it's a gigantic free-for-all water fight. In cities from Bangkok to Chiang Mai, Thais send water balloons and buckets joyfully flying, aim water pistols at passing motorcyclists and túk-túk drivers, and even bring in the odd elephant to drench the crowds.

But the real meaning of Songkran runs deeper. It's a time of new beginnings, when Thais scrub their homes and clean Buddha images, washing away last year's dirt and, hopefully, any sins and bad luck too. It's a time for paying respects to elderly relatives by sprinkling fragrant water on their hands, for giving alms to monks and building sand chedi to raise the levels of temple courtyards.

You can bring a little Songkran into your life any time – it doesn't need to be New Year and you don't need to be a Buddhist. Clean your house, clean your body, resolve to leave any unpleasantness from the past behind you and look forward to a bright and shiny future. Through positive thinking we can achieve clarity and peace of mind, and let the good karma flow.

RESPECT YOUR ELDERS

SECRET SPEND TIME WITH FAMILY TO UNDERSTAND
YOUR CONTEXT

Tradition Tsagaan Sar (White Month)
Date Mongolian New Year (late January to early March)
Celebrated in Mongolia

Leaving home to travel the world and live overseas opens our eyes to the world around us. While it's exciting, this flight from the nest can cause an unhappy separation from our loved ones and create a rift between the new life and the old.

Spending long periods of time away from home can make us forget our commitment to family and the role we play in it. At risk is our past: our traditions and the lessons taught to us by our elders.

The Mongolian New Year is a time for families to reconnect and honour the elder members of the clan. Parents and grandparents are greeted with a clasping of the arms known as a *zolgokh*. This gesture includes the passing of a blue or white silk scarf, representing the clear sky and purity of the soul. Sons, daughters and grandchildren utter words of respect for their elders, recalling their wisdom, compassion and generosity.

The celebration and feast only last a day but the practice of honouring elders – including family friends, teachers and coworkers – continues for weeks afterwards.

A calendar is hardly necessary for carrying out these Mongol rites. Make it a weekly or a monthly practice to reconnect with the elder members of your family. Call if you're far from home or visit if you're nearby.

Spending time to reconnect gives you a sense of place and a better understanding of how and where you fit in with your mob.

TURN THE TABLES ON HISTORY

SECRET EMBRACE THE PAINFUL PAST WITH A LIGHT HEART

Tradition Festival de Diablos y Congos (Festival of the Devils and Congos)

 Date Biennial, two weeks after Carnaval

Celebrated in Portobelo, Panamá

Displacement, enslavement and injustice: these disturbing elements of the human story make us uneasy. Against a past that is ironclad and immutable, we feel powerless. Time passes, paving over these episodes, but does it provide a clean slate?

The truth is, not much good happens when we forget the more distressing lessons of history. When ancestors' stories are lost, so is a culture's sense of identity. After hardship, a narrative of shame and loss becomes the new reality – as oppressive as slavery itself. It takes courage to reckon with the past. And even more to play with it.

In Portobelo, Panamá, the Devils and Congos Festival celebrates cimarrones, black slaves who fled their Spanish colonial masters for the rainforest. In the festival, their descendants, known as Congos, make rebellion and ridicule the order of the day as roles are playfully reversed. So-called slavers travel the crowd 'kidnapping' spectators for outrageous ransoms (though a few coins can purchase your release). Their colourful rags mock the pompous finery of the Spanish elite and their reverse speech emulates ancestors who once spoke mutiny in codes.

Congo art also reclaims identity. Bastones, or painted walking sticks, represent the cimarrones' only weapon for escape and survival. Self-portraits are often framed by broken mirror shards, which both admit damage and pick up the pieces.

These expressions, from art to street theatre, show how to honour the past by reclaiming even its thorny parts. With a light heart, it's possible to revisit hardship. Parody your enemies, but make peace too.

ILLUMINATE YOUR SPIRIT

SECRET **REFRESH YOUR PERSPECTIVE AND SEEK THE GOOD IN LIFE**

Tradition **Diwali or Deepavali (Festival of Lights)**

Date **The new-moon night between mid-October and mid-November**

Celebrated in **India**

Life poses challenges: career setbacks, arguments with a spouse, or a real tragedy such as the death of a loved one. This we know. But sometimes it is essential to recalibrate. We always have the opportunity to recast life's difficulties as learning experiences; we can sweep them clean and start anew.

Circumstances change, but creating an environment of positivity can be a constant.

In India, the holiday of Diwali provides just this opportunity to embrace the triumph of peace over pain, in life and within your spirit, and to start fresh. During the five-day Hindu celebration, people cleanse and prepare to welcome Lakshmi, the Goddess of Good Fortune, into their lives.

Houses and shops are swept and whitewashed. The peak of the festival falls on the new moon, and the country's pitch-black skies are ablaze with fireworks. Row upon glittering row of single-wick lamps line rooftops and window sills.

Through this practice, people embrace the positive in life, celebrating and welcoming Lakshmi and other gods who are bringers of good things, like Hanuman and Ganesha – the Remover of Obstacles and Lord of Auspicious Beginnings.

Bring the spirit of Diwali into your daily life. Clean a room from top to bottom. Feeling ambitious? Pick a wall and paint it a fresh, hopeful colour. And light candles…on window sills, mantles, balconies. Warm your own heart and maybe at the same time share that loving hopefulness and anticipation with someone else.

BE PROUD OF YOUR ROOTS

SECRET EMBRACE YOUR HERITAGE TO BETTER
UNDERSTAND YOURSELF

Tradition Maori haka
Date Any time
Celebrated in New Zealand

The world is homogenising: rather than being made up of individual ingredients, it seems it's one big megastew.

As differences disappear and the world slurries together, we can lose sight of our roots. We no longer feel part of something, and instead we feel lonely and lacking in identity. Reconnecting with our heritage can confer a greater sense of self, not to mention the cosy hug of camaraderie.

Take the Maori. A haka is a traditional Maori form of dance, with many variants – some hakas are war cries, some are welcomes, while still others are ceremonial displays.

Despite its fearsome fist-waving and tongue-poking, 'Kamate Kamate' – the New Zealand All Blacks' iconic prematch spine-tingler – is not a call to arms on the rugby pitch. It celebrates a past chief's evasion of the army sent to kill him, yet this passionate ritual now stands for much more. It is the pride of a nation condensed into a stanza; it unites Kiwis of all backgrounds. And it scares the bejesus out of the opposition…

At the close of 'Kamate', New Zealanders feel uplifted and united. So find your own haka. On a personal scale, ask relatives about their past; too often, we leave this too late. Or consider researching your family tree.

Outside the home, don't be afraid to cheer when your 'team' (village, ethnic group, nation) is up against it. This isn't about nationalism at its flag-waving worst. It's a celebration that helps you feel your kinship with your clan.

KINDNESS TO STRANGERS

As children, we're taught that strangers are dangerous. As adults, we're encouraged to lock our car doors at traffic lights, secure our houses, keep a bristling awareness while walking the streets at night.

Yes, the world can be hostile, but is our culture of fear robbing us of a very simple and heartfelt pleasure – the pleasure of giving help and open welcome to a fellow human being just for the goodness that's involved?

Modern life has drained Islamic hospitality of its full traditional fervour (although you might still find yourself surprised!), but in areas of Central Asia, particularly rural ones, it's still customary to give everything to the guest, even if it's all you have – and even if the guest is a stranger to you. Thus do you honour God.

In Uzbekistan, there is a saying: *mehmon otanda ulugh* – 'the guest is greater than the father'. Traditionally, a host would slaughter a sheep to feed a stranger, offering the visitor the choicest delicacies from the animal's head.

You may find attempts to offer a sheep's eye to the next person you see unsuccessful, but there are plenty of ways that you can extend the hand of selfless friendship to someone you've never met before.

That bemused tourist struggling with tickets, map and an unfamiliar language? Offer them help, and maybe a coffee and some local knowledge. That new guy in your office? Invite him to lunch with a bunch of your friendliest colleagues. Or maybe just give the coat off your back to a charity this winter. It's guaranteed to warm the cockles of your heart!

SAVOUR THE FRUITS OF YOUR LABOUR

SECRET RECOGNISE AND CELEBRATE YOUR ACCOMPLISHMENTS

Tradition **Crop Over**
Date **May to August**
Celebrated in **Barbados, Lesser Antilles**

There's so much to do and rarely enough hours in the day to do it all. Finish one thing and it's on to the next. Blood, sweat and tears? Wipe them away and start on the next task as quick as you can…

With our time-poor lifestyles, any sense of achievement and satisfaction is crushed under the daily grind, and it can be easy to lose any notion of what all our hard work is for.

The Crop Over festival in Barbados is one of the island nation's premier cultural festivals, encompassing all manner of entertainment and heritage events including calypso music, food and drink, parades and partying. The festivities culminate in the Grand Kadooment, a spectacular procession of costumed revellers dancing through the streets.

The festival's origins date back to the 1780s, when plantation workers celebrated the end of the sugar-cane harvest. They too held a procession – of carts bringing in the last loads of the crop – followed by a time of rejoicing for the completion of all their hard work. Crop Over's roots lie in this traditional harvest festival – an occasion to celebrate and enjoy the fruits of one's labour.

You don't have to work in a sugar-cane field or beat a calypso drum to celebrate life's achievements. Just remember to step back every now and then to acknowledge what you've accomplished (sure, even throw your own kind of celebration).

Those tasks can wait a little while longer, and it'll be good for your sense of purpose and self-worth to reflect on how far you've come. Go on – you've earned it.

GET BACK TO BASICS

SECRET **FIND THE ULTIMATE CONTENTMENT IN FRIENDS, FAMILY AND A GOOD BOOK**

Tradition *Hygge* ('cosiness')
Date **Any time, but particularly summer and Christmas**
Celebrated in **Denmark**

To be happy, we're told, we need to join 17 different social-network clubs and tote up our virtual friends on Facebook. But there's something sadly artificial and forced about this kind of 'fun'. There's a superficial satisfaction maybe, but it's all too harried to provide real happiness. Often the greater contentment comes from simplification, from paring pleasures down to their most basic.

The Danes are well aware of this, which is probably why they continually top global happiness surveys. And it's much to do with a concept of their own invention: *hygge*.

Pronounced 'whoo-ger', the word defies direct translation, but evokes a sense of cosiness and inner warmth – like sharing a nice bottle of red around a roaring open fire. Or inviting close friends to a cottage by the sea. It's songs around the tree at Christmas and sizzling sausages on the barbie in summer. There's no stress, no complications – just comfort and a sense of being completely at ease with the world.

Hygge is actually easy to find – you just need to make the time for it. Organise a few days away, off-grid: it doesn't have to be expensive, just gather some friends and find a campsite – perhaps on the coast. Turn off the computer and swap virtual friends for real ones – invite them over for a cuppa and a chat. Or simply curl up on the sofa with a blanket and a good book. There, you're in *hygge* heaven.

CELEBRATE THE DIRTY WORK

SECRET CONTRIBUTE, BE A USEFUL MEMBER OF SOCIETY, IN ORDER TO FEEL PART OF SOMETHING GREATER THAN YOURSELF

Tradition **Mingas (community work days)**
Date **Whenever help is needed**
Celebrated in **Chile**

We are living in the age of the individual. We learn to meet our own needs, swelling with pride as small children when we can announce, 'I did it myself'. Long before we've concocted our first plate of clotted spaghetti on leaving home, self-sufficiency is the dish we savour above all.

Just as we never want to ask for help, sometimes we may be slow to give it. With all the demands that are made on us, it's easy to live in a bubble. But it behoves us to recognise that collaboration can be an equally viable survival skill. Take nature, with its hives of honeybees or the African lioness that pitches in to raise the pride.

On the Chilean archipelago of Chiloe, the *minga* is an event where neighbours offer up their sweat and toil for the feast that follows. The tradition is rooted in the history of these humble fishermen and subsistence farmers who have always had to rely on each other for hard physical labour.

It can mean harvesting potato crops, shingling a barn or even hitching up teams of oxen to put a whole house on logs and then roll it to a new location. In thanks, the host barbecues a whole lamb or gathers up a seafood feast, made even merrier by *chicha* – homemade cider.

What if we brought collective survival into our own lives? Offer yourself up for dirty work. And when you're in need, ask for help with the hard stuff, then reward your friends with the worthiest of celebrations.

CARPE DIEM

Tradition **Mardi Gras (Fat Tuesday)**
Date **47 days before Easter (January/February)**
Celebrated in **New Orleans, USA**

From an early age we are told what we should and shouldn't do. We *should* brush our teeth; we *shouldn't* be rude at the dinner table. We *should* work hard but we *shouldn't* daydream.

The rules, the inhibitions, the fear of what others may think can end up governing our lives.

There are just a few days on the calendar that allow everyone, young and old, to live in the *now*, and New Orleans has one of the best: Mardi Gras. It is a day when we all can wear face paint and skip in the streets as if we were children released from the should-shouldn't prison.

In New Orleans and countries as varied as Brazil, Belgium, France and Senegal, Mardi Gras is the culmination of the Carnival season. It marks the last day before the start of Lenten restrictions, and is often viewed as a day of excess, with liquor and mayhem figuring prominently.

Everyone lets go of their deeper inhibitions, seizing the moment to wear glitter, dance, prance, sing and laugh.

Outside of Mardi Gras, commit to doing one thing each day that makes it your own. You may not feel like wearing a feather boa and rumba-ing down the hall to the water cooler at work, but you could hold a gyrating boogie session in your living room. Wear a bright stripy scarf. Or simply take time out to gaze at the night sky.

This is your day – the past is gone and the future is uncertain – so seize it!

THE TIES THAT BIND

SECRET APPRECIATE THE GIFT OF FAMILY

Tradition Raksha Bandhan

Date Full-moon day in the Hindu month of Shravan (July or August)

Celebrated in India

Growing up, who didn't bicker and fight occasionally with their brothers and sisters? And at some point, who hasn't blamed their parents for all their problems and disappointments?

Even as adults, conflicts with our family members can persist, but as the old adage goes, you can't choose your family. And is it possible you take them for granted? Your family may be a collection of clashing personalities, but they are some of the closest ties you'll have in life. Who else can say they really knew you way back when?

Hindus in India celebrate the brother–sister bond in an annual festival known as Raksha Bandhan, 'the bond of protection'. On this joyful and indulgent day, girls say prayers for their brothers, prepare special foods and ceremoniously tie a *rakhi*, or bracelet, made of cotton or silk on each brother's right wrist. This symbolises affection, love and protection from harm.

In turn, girls are lavished with gifts from their brothers, who bless their sisters and promise to look out for them in the year ahead. For those who don't have brothers and sisters, cousins, aunts and uncles can be honoured in the same way. The practice begins in childhood and continues for life.

Is there something fun or special you can do to acknowledge and show appreciation for someone in your family? A meaningful 'ritual' you could create to celebrate and strengthen your unique bond? While friends may come and go, our family will always be connected to us. They can provide a safe haven and are the source of some of life's most joyful moments.

SHARE YOUR BOUNTY

SECRET GIVE AWAY SOMETHING YOU VALUE TO APPRECIATE
HOW LUCKY YOU ARE

 Tradition *Inati* (sharing)
Date Every day
Celebrated in The Pacific Islands, especially Tokelau & Cook Islands

Me, me, me... That's what it's all about these days.

Any sense of community seems to be fast vanishing as we hunker down behind closed doors, anonymous solo artists rather than group players. Many of us scarcely know our neighbours, let alone consider their well-being. We're all focused on our own progress and needs, making sure 'I'm all right Jack'. This can only lead to an increasingly uncaring, and unhappy, society.

On tiny Tokelau, one of the world's most isolated archipelagos, such individualism isn't an option. Comprising three low-lying and tropically idyllic coral atolls – a 20-hour boat ride from nearest neighbour Samoa – remote Tokelau can only function if its minuscule population works together, with those who have helping those who have not.

Despite increasing influences from the cash-based Western world, on Tokelau the system of *inati* (sharing) is still practised. Every day, the fresh catch is laid out on the beach and the village *taupulega* (council) dishes it out according to who needs it most.

You don't need to be from Tokelau to embrace the principles of *inati*. Start by looking local – are there people in your community who need help? Could you make meals for an elderly neighbour? Or give away the hard-grafted spoils of your vegie patch to friends without gardens (or green fingers)?

Or perhaps it's skills and time you could share. Offer to fix a listing fence or provide assistance with a tax return, and take a moment to realise how fortunate you are to be in the position to offer some help.

IN ALL THINGS, BALANCE

Who doesn't feel they've lost their equilibrium these days?

We work more than we play, and spend more time inside than out. Sitting at a computer all day, it's easy to feel on the verge of burnout.

Today's personal-growth gurus preach self-care, but seeking harmony through balance has long been an Eastern tradition. Cultures across Asia believe the five natural elements – fire, water, earth, metal and wood – are the energy-filled building blocks of the universe.

In Korea, the *obangsaek* (traditional five colours) of red, black, yellow, white and green/blue correspond both to the elements and to our five basic tastes: bitter, salty, sweet, spicy and sour, respectively. By balancing these components in one dish and creating harmony in both colour and taste, you draw power and promote health and happiness.

The principle is well illustrated by the quintessential Korean meal *bibimbap*, in which equal quantities of julienned ingredients such as carrot, dark *pyogo* mushroom, white bellflower root and green water parsley are laid concentrically around a yellow egg yolk on a bowl of rice. It's in the mixing before eating that the whole becomes greater than the parts.

You may not want to spend hours precisely cutting vegetables as a meditative exercise, but it's worth considering which elements of your life are out of balance. Do you go to extremes, spending all your time on your career to the detriment of your relationships? Is your physical or spiritual well-being suffering?

Take a lesson from this colourful cuisine: mixing it up more equally can be a beautiful thing.

COLOUR UP YOUR LIFE

SECRET RELEASE YOUR INNER CHILD AND PLAY

Tradition **Holi**
Date **Phalguna (February/March)**
Celebrated in **India**

We strive. Strive for a good job. Strive for a better job. Strive to buy a house. Strive to pay off the house. Strive to find the love of our life. Strive to solve the meaning of life… Is it *really* any wonder that stress-related ailments are rocketing upwards?

In the heart-racing strive-athon of life, our in-a-hurry inner adult is doing a wonderful job of asphyxiating our inner child, leaving us more frazzled and more disenchanted than ever before.

Feeling strive-athoned out? Hello Holi! This happy Hindu 'Festival of Colours' sees people of all stripes jump off the frenetic treadmill of life to unleash their inner child. And how! Merrymakers playfully douse one another with balloons filled with water and fistfuls of coloured powder to celebrate the onset of spring.

Taking place on auspicious days of Phalguna, this feisty festival is also a time for indulging in delicious *mithai* (Indian sweets) and special Holi *lassi* – an iced-water beverage laced with almonds, pistachios, rose petals or possibly *bhang* (derived from marijuana).

Another component of Holi is the lighting of bonfires to symbolise the demise of Holika, a wicked demoness. It's all about setting negative forces ablaze.

When the strive-athon of life starts wearing you down, why not colour life up, Holi style? A water-balloon fight in the backyard followed by feasting with friends will swiftly wash away pent-up stress.

Or symbolically burn your personal demons by jotting down your worries on scraps of paper, catapulting them into the fireplace and watching your woes disappear in soul-cleansing puffs of (Holi) smoke.

HOW TO BE HUMAN

The cult of the individual is paramount in our Western way of life. All our focus is on ourselves and our own problems or successes. We don't instinctively see ourselves as part of the larger whole, and when we stand alone, we also fall alone.

The distinctly African concept of *ubuntu* is the understanding that no human exists in isolation. It is often translated as 'I am only a person through other people'. *Ubuntu* recognises that everything one does affects others, and that the welfare of each is dependent upon the welfare of all.

This way of thinking makes moral responsibility, generosity and empathy intrinsic. It means that Africans will routinely invite strangers into their homes and feed them when they are hungry. It means that children are raised with the input of a whole village rather than letting parents struggle on their own. And because interdependence works both ways, it means that people are willing to accept help, as well as give it.

This ancient philosophy is celebrated in the Ubuntu Festival, held every July in Cape Town. It's a five-day festival of talks and events about human connections.

Practising *ubuntu* in your own life may be as simple as cultivating empathy. Listen to others, *really* listen, and put yourself in their shoes.

Volunteering your time with a charity at home or abroad is another great way to find that sense of belonging and unity, of being attuned with others. And if you need help, ask for it – you don't have to do it all alone!